I0169132

The Tree
That Saved Connecticut

BY

HENRY FISK CARLTON

Edited by CLAIRE T. ZYVE, Ph.D.
Fox Meadow School, Scarsdale, New York

HOW TO BE A GOOD RADIO ACTOR

The play in this book has actually been produced on the radio. Possibly you have listened to this one when you tuned in at home. The persons whose voices you heard as you listened, looked just as they did when they left their homes to go to the studio, although they were taking the parts of men and women who lived long ago and who wore costumes very different from the ones we wear today.

The persons whose voices you heard stood close together around the microphone, each one reading from a copy of the play in his hand. Since they could not be seen, they did not act parts as in other plays, but tried to make their voices show how they felt.

When you give these plays you will not need costumes and you will not need scenery, although you can easily arrange a broadcasting studio if you wish. You will not need to memorize your parts; in fact, it will not be like a real radio broadcast if you do so, and, furthermore, you will not want to, since you will each have a copy of the book in your hands. All you will need to do is to remember that you are taking the part of a radio actor, that you are to read your speeches very distinctly, and that by your voice, you will make your audience understand how you feel. In this way, you will have the fun of living through some of the great moments of history.

HOW TO FOLLOW DIRECTIONS
IN THE PLAY

There are some directions in this play which may be new to you, but these are necessary, for you are now in a radio broadcasting studio, talking in front of a microphone. The word [*in*] means that the character is standing close to the microphone, while [*off*] indicates that he is farther away, so that his voice sounds faint. When the directions [*off, coming in*] are given, the person speaking is away from the microphone at first but gradually comes closer. The words [*mob*] or [*crowd noise*] you will understand mean the sound of many people talking in the distance.

Both the English and the dialect used help make the characters live, so the speeches have been written in the way in which these men and women would talk. This means that sometimes the character may use what seems to you unusual English. The punctuation helps, too, to make the speeches sound like real conversation; for example, you will find that a dash is often used to show that a character is talking very excitedly.

CAST

GOVERNOR TREAT
LIEUTENANT ALLYN
GOVERNOR ANDROS
CAPTAIN WADSWORTH
COLONEL BLIGH
THE SEXTON
CHARLES WILLYS
VOICE

THE TREE
THAT SAVED CONNECTICUT

ANNOUNCER

In the year 1661 Connecticut received from the hand of Charles the Second a very liberal charter granting to the people of the colony almost complete self-government and to the colony an enormous stretch of territory extending westward to the Pacific Ocean. For fifteen years the colony prospered under the generous charter. Then in 1676 trouble arose with the Governor of New York, Sir Edmund Andros, about the boundary line between the two colonies. Andros demanded authority over all the land west of the Connecticut River. Governor Treat of Connecticut refused to submit. Andros threatened to seize the disputed land. Treat defied him. Andros fitted out three ships, embarked a military force, and set out for Saybrooke, Connecticut. Treat ordered out the militia, garrisoned the fort at Saybrooke, and waited.

Our first scene is in the fort on the morning of July 9, 1676. The Governor is at breakfast when he hears—

VOICE [*distance*]

Sail, ho!

ALL [*closer*]

Sail, ho! Here they come; call the governor [*etc.*]

ALLYN [coming in]

Governor! Governor! The ships are coming into the harbor!

TREAT

Are you certain they are the ships of Governor Andros?

ALLYN

Come and see for yourself, Governor.

TREAT

Come along, then. Lieutenant Allyn, how many ships did you see? [*crowd noises swell up*]

ALLYN

Only one, sir. I didn't wait for any more.

TREAT

Ah, here we are! Give me your hand while I climb to the ramparts.

ALLYN

Yes, sir! Ah! There you are, sir!

TREAT

Good!

ALL [*in*]

There's three of 'em, Governor! That's Andros, sir. No doubt o' that!

TREAT

Yes, yes, three! Andros's ships! That's certain! [*calling*] Every man to his place! Load your muskets and prepare for action! Andros shall not land!

ALL

Aye! We'll stop him! Just let him try it!

Here, give me your ramrod. Have you got an extra flint? [*etc.*]

TREAT

Lieutenant Allyn.

ALLYN

Yes, sir!

TREAT

Load the cannon!

ALLYN

It is loaded, sir.

TREAT

Fire across the bow of the forward ship! Make them come to!

ALLYN

Yes, sir! [*calling*] Throw the cannon across the bow of the forward ship!

VOICE

Yes, sir!

ALLYN

Fire! [*a cannon shot*]

ALL

Oh! Look at it!

Yea! Good shot!

TREAT

Excellent! That will show Andros our temper!

ALLYN

The ship is coming about, sir!

TREAT

So I see! They may be going to answer our shot with a broadside! [*calling*] Down! Every man down behind the ramparts!

ALLYN

Down! Down! Every man down!

VOICE [*distant*]

Ahoy, the fort!

TREAT

Oh! Hailing us! Well, let them hail!

VOICE

Ahoy, the fort!

TREAT

Can you see who it is, Lieutenant?

ALLYN

No, sir!

VOICE

I say there! Ahoy, the fort! Is there anyone there? Answer or we'll open fire on you!

TREAT

Hail them, Lieutenant.

ALLYN [*calling*]

Hello there, what do you want?

VOICE

Is the Governor of Connecticut Colony in the fort?

ALLYN [*low*]

What shall I tell him?

TREAT

Tell him I'm here.

ALLYN [*loud*]

Yes, the Governor is here!

VOICE

Governor Andros sends his compliments—

TREAT [under his breath]

Compliments, indeed!

VOICE

And requests Governor Treat to come aboard for a parley.

TREAT

Never! Tell him if Andros has anything to say let him come here, alone and unarmed, and say it!

ALLYN

Yes, sir! [*loud*] Governor Treat's compliments. He requests Governor Andros to come ashore for a parley.

TREAT

Alone and unarmed.

ALLYN [*loud*]

If he means no harm, let him come alone and unarmed.

TREAT

He'll never come!

ALLYN

They're letting a small boat down, sir!

TREAT

Indeed! Who is in it?

ALLYN

A sailor and another—

TREAT

Andros?

ALLYN

It may be, I don't know him. They're pulling away
from the side now.

TREAT

If that is really Andros, he's a brave man.

ALLYN

Aye, sir, he is that. Will you go down to meet him?

TREAT

Indeed I will, if he has the courage to come ashore
without a guard! I can do no less than meet him at

the shore. Come along, Lieutenant. [*calling*] Stand by, men, ready for action at any moment! Lieutenant Allyn and I are going out to meet the Governor!

ALLYN

Through this portal, sir! I've unlocked it.

TREAT

Thank you.

ALLYN

The boat is just beaching, sir.

TREAT

Good! And here he comes.

ALLYN

Alone!

TREAT

Have I the honor of greeting Governor Andros?

ANDROS [coming in, storming angrily]

What is the meaning of this, sir? What is the meaning of this?

TREAT

I beg your pardon?

ANDROS

This—this show of force? What is the meaning of it, I say?

TREAT

Sir! This force is here to maintain the rights of this colony against the illegal aggression of New York!

ANDROS

Where is your Governor?

TREAT

Here!

ANDROS

Well, Governor, I'll have you know that I have come here in the legal performance of my duties to take command of land legally and lawfully a part of the possessions of His Grace, the Duke of York.

TREAT

I have already informed you, sir, that you shall not have it!

ANDROS

Is this rebellion?

TREAT

It is not, I assure you. But we will hold this land which is ours by right of grant from His Majesty, Charles the Second.

ANDROS

My commission as Governor of this territory comes directly from His Grace, the Duke of York.

TREAT

His Grace has no jurisdiction here.

ANDROS

Here, sir, are my orders. [*rattle of paper*]

TREAT

And here, sir, is a true copy of our charter. [*rattle of paper*]

ANDROS

My orders supersede your charter.

TREAT

Our charter is a royal grant, and cannot be superseded except for cause by due process of law.

ANDROS

I shall take possession under my orders. You can appeal to the Privy Council for redress.

TREAT

You can take possession only after every man in this fort is dead!

ANDROS

Do you still insist on this ridiculous show of force?

TREAT

I do! If you make a move to land your troops, we will open fire!

ANDROS

Very well. I shall report to His Grace that I was prevented from obeying his command by an unwarranted and illegal show of force!

TREAT

And we shall report to His Majesty that we defended our rights under our royal charter.

ANDROS

Confound your charter! I'll see to it that you lose it! Good day, sir.

TREAT

Good day!

ANNOUNCER

So Governor Andros took his departure without gaining possession of the territory he claimed. For the next ten years Connecticut continued in undisputed possession of her charter, and then on December 19, 1686, Andros was appointed Governor of all New England. News of this appointment reached Connecticut several months later.

Our next scene is at the State House in Hartford. It is June of 1687. The General Court of the Connecticut Colony is in session. As our scene opens, Governor Treat is addressing the Assembly.

TREAT

Gentlemen! I have called you here to consider a matter of grave importance to the life of this colony. As you know, His Majesty has seen fit to deprive us of our rights under our charter and has appointed a Governor who is to have supreme power over this colony and all of New England.

WADSWORTH

Your Excellency—

TREAT

Yes, Captain Wadsworth?

WADSWORTH

Let us not submit! Let us appeal to the Privy Council! We have our rights under the charter.

ALL

Yes, yes! Let us not submit!

TREAT

It is useless, gentlemen. When we are ordered to submit, we must submit or be in rebellion.

WADSWORTH

When may we expect the order?

TREAT

I was informed this very morning that an officer of Governor Andros was on his way here to take over the government of the colony, and we might expect him this very day.

WADSWORTH

Then what can we do, sir?

TREAT

We can submit—indeed we must submit to the rule of Governor Andros, but, gentlemen, we must not relinquish our charter!

ALL

No, no! We must save our charter. [*etc.*]

TREAT

But how can we save it? If I am ordered to give it up, what can I do? I have it here. It is in my possession. How can I hold it against an order to relinquish it?

WADSWORTH

Your Excellency, if it is not in your possession, you cannot give it up.

TREAT

But it is, Captain Wadsworth.

WADSWORTH

Then, sir, I move you that this Assembly forthwith take it out of your possession and intrust it to a committee for safe-keeping.

TREAT

Yes, that is possible.

VOICE

Second!

TREAT

You have heard the proposal. Those favoring—

ALL

Aye!

TREAT

Opposed—it is a vote. Will someone propose the committee?

VOICE

Your Excellency, I propose Captain Wadsworth, Charles Willys, and John Talcott.

TREAT

But Talcott is not here.

WADSWORTH

All the better, sir, since we cannot give up the charter except upon unanimous consent of the committee.

TREAT

A very good arrangement. Is there a second to the nomination for the Charter Committee?

VOICE

Second! [*loud knock*]

TREAT

Don't open until we have had the vote! All favoring—

ALL

Aye! [*knocking*]

BLIGH [*outside*]

Open, in the name of the King!

TREAT

Opposed? Carried!

BLIGH [insistent knocking]

Open, open, I say! Open in the name of the King.

TREAT [over the noise]

Captain Wadsworth, I deliver this charter into your hands for safe-keeping.

WADSWORTH

We shall keep it, sir. Never fear!

TREAT [*calling*]

Doorkeeper, open the door!

VOICE

Yes, sir!

BLIGH [coming in]

What is the meaning of this, sir? Why was I locked out?

TREAT

Your pardon, sir. But what authority have you, sir, to break into the Assembly of the General Court of Connecticut?

BLIGH

I have come to take over the government of this colony under the authority of Governor Andros.

TREAT

Indeed, and who are you, if we may be permitted to know?

BLIGH

Ah, of course—I have the honor to be Samuel Bligh, Colonel in His Majesty's service. Are you Robert Treat?

TREAT

I am.

BLIGH

Here are your orders! [*rattle of paper*]

TREAT

Thank you. "Hereby ordered"—yes—yes—"in compliance with mandate of His Majesty"—yes, indeed. Colonel Bligh, we are ready to turn the government over to Governor Andros.

BLIGH

Then, sir, you will deliver up the charter to me.

TREAT

What?

BLIGH

The charter! The charter—read the rest of the order, sir.

TREAT [*reading*]

"Governor Treat is hereby ordered to deliver up the forfeited charter"—but, Colonel Bligh, I cannot deliver up the charter—

BLIGH

Why not?

TREAT

Because, sir, it is not in my possession.

BLIGH

In whose possession is it?

TREAT

It has been intrusted by the General Court to a special committee.

BLIGH

Indeed—and who comprises the committee?

TREAT

The clerk will read the names of the committee.

ALLYN

May it please you, sir, the committee consists of Captain Wadsworth, Charles Willys, and John Talcott.

BLIGH

Are any of those named here?

WADSWORTH

Yes, sir!

BLIGH

Your name, sir?

WADSWORTH

Captain Wadsworth.

BLIGH

Captain Wadsworth, I order you to deliver up the charter to me.

WADSWORTH

Oh, yes, and have you an order for it there?

BLIGH

Indeed I have. Governor Treat has just read it.

WADSWORTH

May I be allowed to see it?

BLIGH

Of course. Governor Treat, will you let this gentleman read the order and be satisfied.

WADSWORTH [rattle of paper]

Hm, yes.—"Governor Treat—hereby ordered"—but, Colonel, this is an order upon Governor Treat!

BLIGH

Of course it is! Now are you satisfied?

WADSWORTH

I am deeply sorry, sir, I do not see how the committee can comply with this order.

BLIGH

Why not, pray—is it not properly signed and
sealed?

WADSWORTH

Oh yes. Signed properly, but it is drawn against the
Governor—and not against the Charter Committee.

BLIGH

Why—what—oh, this is too much! Governor
Andros warned me that you would be stubborn and
stiff-necked! But I'll have that charter! Here—I'll
change that order—give it here!

WADSWORTH

Here you are, sir. [*rattle of paper*]

BLIGH

Hm—yes—a quill. So—now—"The Charter
Committee—is hereby ordered"—there you are.
Now I hope you are satisfied.

WADSWORTH

Are you satisfied with this, Governor?

TREAT

Hm—does this not seem to be a forgery, Captain
Wadsworth?

WADSWORTH

It not only seems to be, sir, but it is. I saw him make an illegal change in the order. All of us saw it.

ALL

Yes, yes! We saw him.

It is a forgery! Don't obey it!

TREAT

I should say that the change invalidated the entire order!

BLIGH

What? You are trying to put me in the wrong?

WADSWORTH

Not at all, sir! You have put yourself in the wrong.

BLIGH

But—but—you forced me to make that change in the order.

TREAT

I believe, Colonel, we merely pointed out that your order was inadequate; we did not force you to commit forgery.

BLIGH

Oh, this is a trick! This is a trick! I demand the immediate surrender of the government and the charter!

TREAT

What is the will of the Assembly? Can we deliver up the government under an order which is obviously forged?

ALL

No, no! No indeed!

TREAT

The vote is against you, Colonel.

BLIGH

Andros will come himself and attend to this affair. I wash my hands of it! He'll make you pay for this day's work—and he'll get the charter! Good day!

ALL

Good day!

ANNOUNCER

Andros did come, as Colonel Bligh had threatened, but not for several months. But when he came, he came in state, with a company of soldiers, two trumpeters, and Colonel Bligh. He intended this time to get the charter, and no mistake!

Governor Treat called the General Court to assemble on the evening of October 31, 1687, to confer with Governor Andros and make one last determined stand to retain the charter even if there was no way to retain their rights under the charter.

Our next scene is at the State House in Hartford. It is evening. The sexton is preparing the room for the meeting which is about to take place.

SEXTON [to himself]

Now these candles, where'd I best put 'em. I cal'ate mebbe I'd better scatter 'em around the room—

WADSWORTH [*coming in*]

Good even to you, Nathan.

SEXTON

Even, Captain Wadsworth. Even, Master Allyn.

ALLYN

Good even, Nathan.

WADSWORTH

These candles, Nathan.

SEXTON

Yes, sir! I was jest a puttin' 'em around where everybody'd git a little light.

WADSWORTH

I think perhaps you'd best put them all on the Governor's table.

SEXTON

The Governor's table. Yes, sir! So—one here—and one—

ALLYN

No, no, Nathan. Put them all together at this end of the table.

SEXTON

This end by the window?

ALLYN

I think that will be best, don't you, Captain?

WADSWORTH

Of course! The Governor needs a great deal of light.

SEXTON

But, sir, the draft from the window—it may blow them out.

ALLYN

Well, well, if it does, Nathan, we'll just have to light them all again.

SEXTON

Yes, sir! Of course, sir!

WADSWORTH [*low*]

Now Allyn, seeing you are the clerk of the General Court, you can sit at the Governor's table without exciting suspicion.

ALLYN

Yes, Captain!

WADSWORTH

Best put your chair next the window.

ALLYN

Have you the charter?

WADSWORTH

Yes, I have it with me, and when Andros demands it I shall have to produce it.

ALLYN

Andros must not be allowed to get his hand on it.

WADSWORTH

That will be your duty.

ALLYN

Yes?

WADSWORTH

Willys will be waiting outside that window, next your chair. When the candles go out, grab the charter and toss it out the window. He'll put it in a safe place.

ALLYN

Where?

WADSWORTH

You know the oak in front of his house?

ALLYN

Indeed yes!

WADSWORTH

There is a hollow—high up—

ALLYN

Good!

WADSWORTH [*louder*]

Nathan!

SEXTON

Yes, Captain!

WADSWORTH

A good fire you have in the fireplace.

SEXTON

I figgered to have a good fire—it's a mite chilly this evenin'.

WADSWORTH

It may get overly warm in here before the meeting is over.

SEXTON

Aye.

WADSWORTH

I want you to stand close to that window behind John Allyn's chair.

SEXTON

Yes, sir!

WADSWORTH

Don't leave it. And the moment I say, "Sexton, it's warm in here," throw open the window. You understand?

SEXTON

"Sexton, it's warm in here," throw it open. Yes, sir, I understand.

WADSWORTH

Never mind what anyone else says. Throw it open on my signal and throw it wide open.

SEXTON

But the candles, sir—they may go out. They're right close to the window.

WADSWORTH

Never mind the candles.

SEXTON

Never mind them—yes, sir! [*trumpets sound outside*]

ALLYN

Here comes Andros. Throw open the door.

WADSWORTH

Never mind, Nathan. I'll do it. You stay by that window.

SEXTON

The window. Yes, sir!

WADSWORTH

Enter, Governor Andros.

ANDROS

Thank you. Governor Treat—I now call you that for the last time—will you show me to my place?

TREAT

Of course, sir. Captain Wadsworth, will you usher us to our places?

WADSWORTH

Right this way, Governor. We have arranged this place for you.

ANDROS

Thank you. Do we need all the candles here?

WADSWORTH

For you and the clerk. [*noise and confusion of members entering*]

ANDROS

Yes, yes! Of course! Treat, will you sit at my left?

TREAT

Thank you, sir!

ANDROS

Will you call the Assembly to order?

TREAT

Gentlemen, will you take your places. [*sound of gavel*] The Assembly will please come to order! [*quiet*] In accordance with the command of His Majesty we are met here to surrender the government of the Connecticut Colony to the Royal Governor, Sir Edmund Andros. On behalf of this Assembly, I have the honor, sir, to welcome you and assure you of our submission to His Majesty's command. We have ever been a loyal and a law-abiding people. We surrender the prerogatives of government under our charter with regret; but His Majesty commands, and we, his loyal subjects, have nought to do but obey. We are, sir, yours to command.

ALL [*cheers*]

ANDROS

Thank you, Master Treat. I am agreeably pleased at the expression of obedience. In the name of His Majesty I hereby take command of the colony of Connecticut and order it joined to the colony of Massachusetts Bay, of which you shall henceforth be a part. And now, you have only to surrender the charter to me to complete the ceremony of submission to the order of His Majesty.

TREAT

But, sir, we have signified our submission. The surrender of the charter is quite another thing.

ANDROS

How so?

TREAT

It was granted in perpetuity, to be forfeited only through due process of law.

ANDROS

Have you not been informed, sir, that a writ of quo warranto issued in the proper courts of England was tried and went by default last February?

TREAT

Last February? Indeed, sir! We had no knowledge that any action was brought against it. Who was the complainant?

ANDROS

I was!

TREAT

You, sir?

ANDROS

Indeed, you seem to have forgotten an occasion when I promised you I'd get your charter.

TREAT

No, sir! Unfortunately I still remember it!

ANDROS

I have here the original court order, declaring your charter forfeit, and I shall now trouble your Charter Committee to produce the original document.

TREAT

One moment, sir. Has not every Englishman a right to defend his case before a court of law?

ANDROS

Of course—you had such a chance and failed to appear.

TREAT

We had no notice of the action.

ANDROS

That's not my fault.

TREAT

The court is in error, and we shall appeal.

ANDROS

Appeal all you like; but produce the charter.

TREAT

We do so under protest.

ANDROS

Ah, very well. I care not how much you protest. Once I get the charter, I can assure you, you'll never see it again.

TREAT

But, sir!

ANDROS

Produce the charter.

TREAT

Captain Wadsworth, place the charter on the table.

WADSWORTH

Here it is, sir.

ANDROS

Ah—at last!

TREAT

One moment, sir.

ANDROS

What now?

TREAT

Will you first sign the receipt for the charter, so that the committee may be protected?

ANDROS

Why, certainly, if you wish. It's no matter; but I'll do it. Give me your quill, clerk.

ALLYN

Here you are, sir—and paper.

ANDROS

Yes. Hm—"received—charter—signed"—there—

WADSWORTH

Sexton, it's warm in here!

SEXTON

Yes, sir! [*noise of window*]

ANDROS

Hey, the lights! Quick, what's happened? Lights! Lights!

ALL

The candles have all blown out!

Put down the window!

What's the matter—[*etc.*] [*exclamations continue through the scene*]

ANDROS

Put that window down! What are you trying to do?

SEXTON

Why, sir, it was warm.

ANDROS

Put it down, I say! Light those candles! What foolishness is this? Light those candles, I say! Do you hear me?

SEXTON

Yes, sir, at once, sir! [*noise of window going down*]

Here, sir, I'll light the candles. I'm right sorry, sir. Now, where did I put my flint? Ah, here it is. There you are, sir. I'm right sorry I put you out, sir. I didn't think—

ANDROS

Fool! Now, Treat, hand me the charter.

TREAT

The charter—why, sir—you had it.

ANDROS

Had it? What are you talking about?

TREAT

Why, sir! I saw you put your hand on it the moment
the lights went out.

ANDROS

Indeed I did not. Give it here!

TREAT

But, sir—

ANDROS

Hey—you—Captain—

WADSWORTH

Sir!

ANDROS

Wadsworth, give me the charter!

WADSWORTH

But, sir, I gave it to you.

ANDROS

You did not!

WADSWORTH

But I have here your receipt for it!

ANDROS

Give me back that receipt!

WADSWORTH

I shall certainly do nothing of the kind, sir. I gave you the charter; you gave me this receipt for it. I have here twenty witnesses to the transaction!

ANDROS

I'm being tricked! I say I will have that charter. It's somewhere here, and I'll have it. [*calling*] Colonel Bligh!

BLIGH [*distance*]

Yes, sir!

ANDROS

Surround this place with your soldiers. Don't let a single man leave until he has been searched!

TREAT

Sir, this is illegal! You have no search warrants!

ANDROS

Indeed! I'll do it whether it's legal or not. I'll have that charter, I tell you, if I have to search every spot in this town! I'll have it, I say I'll have it.

ANNOUNCER

And so the great search began. All that night and into the next day the Governor, the Colonel, and their soldiers searched high and low for the missing charter. At last they came to the house of Charles Willys, in front of which stood the great oak in which the charter lay safely hidden.

ANDROS

Who lives here?

TREAT

This is the home of Charles Willys!

ANDROS

Indeed! One of the Charter Committee, eh?

TREAT

Yes, sir!

ANDROS

Good! Search this place inside and out, Colonel. Don't leave a thing unturned.

BLIGH

Very good, sir! Search this place, Captain—thoroughly. Tear up the floors, dig up the garden, rip the upholstery off the furniture, but find that charter!

VOICE

Yes, sir. Follow me!

ANDROS

Bring out the master of the house. The rest of you back up against this tree and don't move!

TREAT

Sir, I protest again—

ANDROS

Protest all you like. It will do you no good until you produce that charter.

TREAT

I don't know where it is. You had it, that's all I know. If you lost it, it is not our fault.

ANDROS

Silence!

BLIGH [a little distance]

Here's the master of the house, sir.

ANDROS

Ah, indeed! Are you Master Willys?

WILLYS

I am.

ANDROS

Where is the charter?

WILLYS

Your pardon, sir, but how should I know?

ANDROS

You were a member of the Charter Committee, were you not?

WILLYS

I was!

ANDROS

Then where is it?

WILLYS

I am informed that the charter—

ANDROS

Yes?

WILLYS

Was placed—

ANDROS

Yes—yes—

WILLYS

In your hands!

ANDROS

Sir! If you don't tell me where that charter is—

WILLYS

What then, sir?

ANDROS

Do you see this oak tree?

WILLYS

I'm not blind, sir.

ANDROS

I'll have you strung up—strung up in it, sir; I'll have
you strung up in it!

WILLYS

I should hate to have such a fine tree perverted to
such a purpose, sir!

ANDROS

Ah! You would! Colonel Bligh! Colonel!

BLIGH [*distance*]

Yes, Governor!

ANDROS

Send me half a dozen soldiers and a stout rope!

BLIGH

Yes, sir!

ANDROS

Ah! Now perhaps we'll get something from you. Will you tell me or will you be hanged by your thumbs from that stout limb up there until you are ready to tell me where the charter is?

TREAT

Governor Andros, I fear you have forgotten yourself in your rage. Master Willys is entitled to a trial before any such punishment can be meted out to him.

ANDROS

Silence, or I'll have you strung up with him! Gad, sir, I'll fill this oak tree with stiff-necked rebellious Connecticut men, but I'll have that charter!

BLIGH

Here are your men, sir!

ANDROS

Good! One of you climb that oak tree. Here, you, Sergeant.

VOICE

Yes, sir!

ANDROS

Give him a hand there. [*sound of starting to climb the tree*] Have the men found anything in the house, Colonel?

BLIGH

Not a thing, sir!

WADSWORTH

Look here, sir.

ANDROS

Ah, Captain Wadsworth. Have you something to say?

WADSWORTH

I have, sir.

ANDROS

Speak out.

WADSWORTH

Tell those men to stay out of that tree and I'll tell you.

ANDROS

All right, Sergeant, come down. I thought we'd get something out of them if we scared them. Well, Captain?

WADSWORTH

Sir, you have lost the charter; that is clear.

ANDROS

Where is it?

WADSWORTH

Just a minute. You have lost it. You also have given us your receipt for it; therefore you should have it.

ANDROS

And I intend to have it.

WADSWORTH

You can't. I can assure you of that, but here is what I propose. The committee is willing to turn over the receipt to you if you will stop this foolish and destructive search for something you can't find.

ANDROS

Never! Sergeant, go up that tree again. We'll string these fellows up.

WADSWORTH

Ah, very well, then. But, sir, you'll look very foolish when you report to the Privy Council that you did not get the charter, and we produce your signed receipt!

ANDROS

What?—Hm—

TREAT

Yes, indeed, Governor. How will you explain that to the King?

ANDROS

What? Why! Ah—very well then, give me the receipt and I'll leave. After all, your charter will do you no good. It's revoked.

TREAT

Exactly! That's a very sensible view to take, Governor Andros. I congratulate you.

WADSWORTH

Here is the receipt, sir.

ANDROS

Humph!

WADSWORTH

You're very welcome, sir.

ANDROS

Colonel Bligh, draw up your guard and prepare to return to Boston. [*orders and confusion*]

TREAT [over the noise]

My congratulations, Captain Wadsworth. A good bargain.

WADSWORTH

Indeed it was. Another foot up the tree, and the Sergeant would have had the charter.

BLIGH

Quick step, march!

ANNOUNCER

By saving the charter Connecticut preserved her claim to separate government, and in 1694 the King decided that the charter was in full legal force. It served as the fundamental order of Connecticut government down to the Revolution and until 1818, when a new state constitution superseded it.

The oak in which the charter was so well hidden was called from that time the "Charter Oak." It stood until August 21, 1856, when it fell. At sunset of that day the bells of Hartford tolled, and mourning was displayed for the historic old tree. And today interested tourists may see the spot where the Charter Oak stood and see a piece of the old tree in the State House.

www.ingramcontent.com/pod-product-compliance
Lightning Source LLC
Chambersburg PA
CBHW031613040426
42452CB00006B/509